TO MARRAKECH
BY AEROPLANE

Other books by Stephen Davis include *Bob Marley* (1983), *Hammer of the Gods* (1985), *Say Kids! What Time Is It?* (1987), *Jajouka Rolling Stone* (1993), *Old Gods Almost Dead* (2001), *Jim Morrison* (2004), *Watch You Bleed* (2008), and *LZ-'75* (2010).

TO MARRAKECH
BY AEROPLANE

Stephen Davis

Inkblot

Copyright © 2010 Stephen Davis
All rights reserved
1st printing

ISBN 0 934301 54 9

Cover Photo: Place Jemaa-el-fna,
Marrakech, Morocco, circa 1911
Cover design: hexit/mjk brooklyn, ny

Published by Inkblot Publications
Providence, Rhode Island

Distributed worldwide by Aftermath Books
Providence, Rhode Island
www.aftermathbooks.com

BARAKA L'AUFIC & CHOUKRAN

Thanks to Joel Rubiner and the staff at Four Winds in Marrakech. Thanks to Abdelatif, Mustapha, Othman, Driss and Moulay. Thanks to Theo, Adele and Dijon at Inkblot. Thanks to my family: Judith, Lily, India and Penny. Thanks to Royal Air Maroc and Royal Air Inter. And to the discarnate spirits of Brion Gysin, Paul Bowles and William S. Burroughs. *Sequiturque patrem, non possibus aequis.*

FOREWORD

In the spring of 2008 I spent some time in Marrakech, the old desert capital of Morocco. I'd first visited "Le Rouge," the red-walled former caravan terminus at the edge of the Sahara, thirty years before. Like Winston Churchill and many others, I kept coming back as often as I could.

I wrote in a notebook while I was there, and then typed up the notes as a gift to my host in the city's ancient medina. I showed this text to my friend and worthy constituent Theo Green, who thought it might be of some interest to readers who share our affinities with the Beat fathers – Bowles, Gysin, Burroughs – who journeyed to Morocco before us.

In addition, none of the postcards I sent from Marrakech on that visit ever reached their destinations. The postage had been an extortionate 14 dirhams – almost two dollars – per card. This text attempts to make up for this lapse.

To Marrakech by Aeroplane is hereby dedicated to the people of that wonderful city, and especially to the mystical spirit of the Jmaa el Fna.

-S.D

5/3/08:

A mauve desert pigeon stares at me from atop the satellite dish on the roof of the house next door. It's six o'clock in the evening, on the edge of the Sahara. The dry blue sky is beginning to turn pink as the sun sinks behind the Atlas Mountains. The breeze comes up, and a peppery smell of grilling meat is borne on the smoke of braziers and kitchens open to the sky. I'm presently alone in my old friend Johar's house in the ancient medina of 21st century Marrakech, waiting for him to arrive from Paris. His connecting plane from Arizona was late to JFK airport in New York last night, and Royal Air Maroc closed our 8:20 flight to Casablanca at 7:30. Johar rang my cell phone and said he was right there, at the gate, but no one else was getting on this flight. Already on board the half-full jet, I tried to protest, but the airline's purser insisted there were serious security issues involving late-arriving luggage. So Johar missed the plane, and was re-booked through Paris.

The Atlantic crossing was a smooth night flight on a Boeing 767. Also aboard was a surgical team from New Jersey – a dozen young docs and nurses – some wearing "Morocco '08" shirts over their green scrubs. They slept soundly as I watched dawn break over the coast of North Africa from eight miles high.

The Casablanca airport used to look like a B-17 aerodrome from World War 2, with herds of goats munching grass by the runways. Now the new terminal is a gleaming architectural statement of Morocco's 21st century pride. Same thing in Marrakech, after a twenty-minute Royal Air Inter flight on a 737: the once-sleepy airport, out near the Menara oasis, used to look as if it were waiting for Antoine de St. Exupery to fly in with the evening mail. The new Menara terminal is now a shining steel arc that looks like a gleaming glass Zeppelin hanger.

Naturally, no luggage of mine made the connection to Marrakech, but two of Johar's people – Driss and Moulay Mohammed – were (thankfully) waiting for me at nine in the morning, beyond the customs exit. My old friend Driss has become more devout since my last visit, in 2001, and now wears a beard and traditional clothes. Moulay Mohammed, about 40, is a high school teacher who moonlights as a customs broker. Both work for Johar's firm, which manufactures beautifully decorated leather goods in classic Moorish style and retails them at high-end rodeos and horse shows in the American Southwest. Johar employs a great crew of local artisans, all of them characters, some of them kif smokers, and he conducts business from a modest house in Derb Sidi Manaraf, deep in the thousand-year-old medina.

Moulay Mo at the wheel of a weathered Fiat, we fly out of the airport and into a new world of vast condo and hotel projects. I'd seen this incredible sprawl of new construction from the 737 as it descended over Marrakech. The old city's edge-of-Sahara environs are being transformed into a Palm Springs for northern Europe. But the vast olive groves and citrus estates between aerodrome and *Centre Ville* are still there, and after a few minutes the immense red walls of Le Rouge come into view and then we're into the dusty morning traffic of a teeming North African metropolis.

Through the massive red city wall via Bab Kechiche, up the rue Bab El Khemis and into the dusty square called Place Moukef, where we leave the car and walk two minutes into the medina's steep-walled alleys. Driss's key lets us into Johar's place, a refurbished old courtyard house with a tiled fountain, modern kitchen and bathroom, and a wonderful view of the Koutoubia mosque's iconic minaret from the roof. I crash out in the salon for a few hours, waiting the arrival of my luggage and my friend – *Insha'Allah* – later that day.

The call to prayer from the nearby Ben Youssef mosque wakes me around five o'clock. Half a dozen mosques serve this densely populated working class district, and the low, growling drones of the various muezzins, amplified by loudspeakers, mosh up with each other to make for five solid minutes of sonorous devotion. Up on the roof I have an outdoor shower, and listen to a baby crying next door and the ruckus of kids playing soccer in the street below. Kites and starlings whiz by my head as I dry off. The sky reddens in the west. A huge marabou stork flies over. The baby is laughing now. Another stork, then another.

Three hours later, Driss and Moulay Mohammed arrive for the drive back to the airport. On the way to the car, they park me in a dark doorway next to a barber while they duck into a mosque to pray. I stand quietly for 15 minutes and watch the passing parade of laden donkeys, mule-powered wagons, girls riding motor scooters, aged locals in white jellabas, and young men wearing denim and baseball caps. From the apartments above come the radio sounds of

Morocco tonight: *Chaabia* pop, *Andaluz* classics, razor-sharp hip-hop from the slums of Casablanca. Someone is roasting chickens down the alley behind me, and the scent of garlic, cumin and oil fills the air.

The new Menara airport terminal by night is a crystal palace of brilliant white light. Moulay Mohammed helps me claim my bag, which had arrived from Casa a few hours after its owner. Johar may be in Paris, might be in Casablanca, could be in the air above the Straits of Gibraltar. We don't know because he's not answering his phone. We watch the flights arriving from London, Frankfurt, Madrid, Paris: hundreds of European visitors, most dressed for a holiday. Still no Johar. I repair to the upstairs café bar overlooking the immense terminal and drink a couple of Flags, the delicious Moroccan lager. A crowded flight from Paris disgorges two hundred passengers, but Johar is not among them. We're about to give up when the last Royal Air Inter flight of the evening arrives from Casablanca. Driss's phone rings. After four hours of waiting, and 30 hours in transit, Johar has arrived.

We wait some more. Driss's phone rings again. There's a problem at customs, since Johar is importing Chinese turquoise and red coral from India for his leather business. While I wait, Moulay Mohammed dives into the customs area to sort this out. Ten minutes later he returns and asks me for 400 dirhams – about $50 – to take care of the customs agents.

Two hours later, well after midnight, Johar and I sit on the darkened roof terrace of his house. The wind is up, and giant royal palms clack their fronds in the breeze. The Koutoubia tower is illumined by klieg lights. Johar has some stale kif left in his mutwi from his last visit, and we pass the sebsi back and forth until dawn, when the muezzins renew their chanting and the faint glow of the sun rising in the east signals that it is time for us to draw this long, inter-continental day to a close.

#

5/4/08

I sleep until noon in the back bedroom. The desert heat is intense. Old friend Ahmed, who does metal work for Johar, arrives with a plastic-wrapped ball of fresh kif, which goes well with coffee, yogurt and cold Sidi Ali bottled water for breakfast. We decamp for the Jmaa el Fna a bit later for newspapers and more coffee. The legendary old town square – once the northern terminus for salt and slave caravans from Niger and Mali – became a bus station in the

20th century. Now the government has banned both cars and busses from the square, and the vast area is even washed down every morning to provide hygienic conditions for the dozens of outdoor cook-shops and grills that draw thousands of locals and tourists to their lamp-lit tables every evening. As recently as eighty years ago, the tortured bodies of criminals and rebels were displayed here, so Jmaa el Fna translates both as "Square of the Dead" and "Place of the Executed."

Back at Derb Sidi Manaraf, Johar and I catch up. He tells me the harrowing tale of how he finally bought this house after many years of renting in various sections of the medina. The property needed total restoration, a job that Johar entrusted to one of his local friends, a smiling rogue of old acquaintance named Abdelatif Zanaqi. Abdelatif then squandered most of the renovation budget on various get-rich-quick schemes and gambling. A year ago, dodging the angry people he owed money to, he locked himself in Johar's unfinished house and refused to come out. One night, the neighbors heard terrible screams, and found Abdelatif writhing in the street, blood foaming from his mouth, in unspeakable agony. He died in the hospital that night, having swallowed sulfuric acid. Then Johar learned that Abdelatif had been in cahoots with Johar's business manager, and that money was missing from the firm as well as from the house budget. It took Johar another year, a river of tears, complicated negotiations with two local families, and many more thousands of dirhams to make the house ready to live in. (In fact, a year later the re-construction of inferior work under the late Zanaqi was still going on.)

"At least that fellow didn't die in your house," the neighbors told Johar, by way of a quantum of solace. They told Johar that he would have had to hire a troupe of Gnawa musicians to perform an all-night exorcism of the malevolent djinns that such a violent death would attract to the premises. Animals would have to be sacrificed, with more blood spilt. The ghastly episode sounded like a sinister, mid-period Paul Bowles short story.

My original idea for this journey was actually to persuade Johar to leave Marrakech and travel north with me. Back in the mid-1970s, he and I were involved with the Master Musicians of Jajouka as both journalists and friends. We had spent many months in the mountains with the semi-famous tribal musicians, who a few years earlier had played with Brian Jones, founder of the Rolling Stones. The subsequent album of the recordings Mr. Jones made in Jajouka is seen by some as the alpha recording of the so-called World Music movement. In 1974, Johar issued his own recordings of the band, a historic document that presented the Jajouka musicians without the sonic distortion – "phasing," etc. – that had been deployed to make Brian Jones's 1968 tapes sound more "far out."

Over the years, the older musicians died out, and Jajouka devolved into what Bob Marley called "ism and schism." Our last visit to the Jebala hills, south of Tangier, where Jajouka perches on the side of Owl Mountain, was in 1989. This was when Bernardo Bertolucci was shooting *The Sheltering Sky* in Tangier, and some of the musicians were featured in the film. Once we arrived up in the hills, we found two groups of musicians who weren't speaking to each other, and we soon left in a state of resigned heartbreak and flew to Marrakech, where Johar had a nice little house with a banana tree growing in the courtyard.

Now, in his new house, Johar and I pondered our options. We were comfortable here in the south, and everyone seemed pleased to see us. Johar had business to attend to, and I was a burnt-out case on a serious kif holiday. We were both sixty years old, not thirty. But still, the lure of

Jajouka is very enticing for anyone who has been exposed to the wild pipes of Pan echoing across the "little blue hills" (as Brion Gysin saw them) of the Jebala, all the way to Chaouan. And also, I wanted to see newly groovy Tangier. In the late 20th century, the old city was a neglected slum under the old king, Hassan II, who hated the decadent town. But now Tangier is a revived and thriving cosmopolitan port, Morocco's gateway to Europe, inhabited by a new generation of Moroccans and expatriates under the semi-benign gaze of the current sultan, Mohammed VI. I'd heard that the recent, and criminally unchecked, development of the area around Tangier has a luridly obscene quality, with some of the new buildings already falling down. But the medina and Kasbah are intact, and some of the mystery of the old place survives. This, at least, is what they say about Tangier here.

Finally, we decided to stay in Marrakech after someone we trusted e-mailed us that Jajouka was so divided into factions that it "feels like Palestine up there." There were stories of violence, vandalism, tribal war. I brewed mint tea, and we spoke about the old musicians we'd revered – Jnuin, Fudul, Skirken, Malim Ali, Malim Ashmi, Mohammed Stitu, Brion Gysin – and our great luck at having witnessed some of the glory days of the Master Musicians of Jajouka.

Late in the day, we headed out again through the tunnel-like passage of Derb Sidi Manaraf and blended with the foot traffic that competed with mules, donkeys and buzzing motorbikes in the bigger street. We stopped at the spice market – crowded with groups of Asian tourists – and ducked into a silver shop that displayed some very cool Tuareg rings in its vitrine. I like to buy "writing rings" when I start a new project, and had just lost two superior examples – a turquoise Hopi double thunderbird, plus a chunky silver Scottish lion-and-thistle ring – the same week I handed in the manuscript of my most recent book. Here in the spice market, we found some simple but stunning variations of the diamond-like Southern Cross motif with which the Tuareg decorate their jewelry and craft. I acquired three rings, kept one, and gave the others as presents to Johar for him and his lovely wife, Conga.

We dined at Chez Chegrouni, the venerable restaurant across from the Qessabine mosque, close to the Jmaa el Fna. I ate savory chicken baked with lemons, raisons and almonds. Johar had a tagine of vegetables. Horse-drawn carriages clopped by, carrying Moroccan families into the upper reaches of the medina. Flashbulbs were going off. The bright lights of the newsstand across the way illumined the little girls begging at the door of the mosque. The square was crowded and smoking with grilling fish and searing meat. We could hear a Gnawa band banging away on their metal castanets across the square. The tagines were delicious, their meaty juices sopped up by warm rounds of fresh bread. We would have lingered a bit, but a French family with young children wanted our table on the terrace, so we split the scene and left it clean, as they used to say in Philadelphia.

Both somewhat jet-lagged, we walked back to Johar's house. A professional guardian was sitting outside his door, having been engaged by Johar (to the delight of the neighbors) to chase off the local teenage riff-raff who otherwise used the dark passage to drink wine and sniff glue all night. We talked until late, passing the sebsi. Johar was playing CDs by Manu Chao, the Barcelona rock star who channels Bob Marley via the Grateful Dead. The music has a beat, you can shake to it, but for me it's not really happening unless you were there, at some Ecstasy-fueled Ibizan rave, in 2001.

The muezzins called the faithful to their prayers at midnight. I went off to bed, and read Sir Walter Scott's *Ivanhoe* until I fell asleep.

Feral cats, copulating loudly on a nearby roof, woke me at three in the morning. I padded down the stone steps and stood in the open courtyard. It felt like a castle from *Ivanhoe*. The sky seemed clear, but somehow starless. The sleeping desert city was restless but quiet. I lit a lamp in Johar's office, and smoked a few pipes of kif while waiting for sleep, which finally came at the dawn call to prayer. My last conscious thought was that it was wonderful to be in a city both hyper-modern and so utterly medieval as well.

Monday May 5th.
I scrambled six fresh eggs, with some flakes of goat cheese, in melted fresh butter and sputtering olive oil for Johar and Driss, and was pleased to get a compliment from Driss, who was once a Moroccan rocker but is now a devout Moslem with a beard, a young family, and a more serious outlook on life. Johar fired up the coffee machine, and I showered on the roof in my bathing suit, in case anyone was looking down on our terrace from the towering sandstone minaret of the nearby Ben Yousseff mosque. Later in

the morning, after the call to prayer, there was a mesmeric half hour of a young man reciting Koranic verses over the mosque's loudspeakers. It was beautiful and inspiring to hear the old Arabic cadences wafting over the red city.

Blinding daylight. Atlas's mountains are hidden by dust and haze. A parliament of birds rules over the medina. Unfixed male cats prowl the interconnected medina rooftops like swaggering little tigers.

Lovely solitude. No stress. I boiled some more eggs. A resinous and fragrant ball of fresh kif arrives at mid-afternoon, with a smile and a nod. The house's thick walls shelter us from the heat. Johar tells me that it took more than six years to buy the house, and then finally obtain the deed and title to the land it sits on.

May 6th.
Sleepless at one o'clock in the morning, grooving on kif and a fiery liqueur called Mahia, distilled from fresh figs and dates by Moroccan Jews near Tangier. It tastes like the anise moonshine from the south of France, Ricard or pastis. I was pleasantly toasty after three small glasses.

Earlier, late afternoon: Ahmed came by with his little boy, Achmido, and we sipped chilled orange juice and smoked a sebsi or three. Stoned silly, I put a big brass bucket on my head and staggered around, which made the little boy laugh. Ahmed is a small, dark Berber craftsman of serious mien, who makes artful metal buckles for the firm. He is soulful and quiet, always has great kif, and is relaxing to have around.

As the sun began to descend over Marrakech, Johar and I walked to the Jmaa el Fna. We had drinks in the bar of the new, incongruously upscale Hotel Les Jardins de la Koutoubia, which occupies the site of an old family palace. The swanky bar was empty except for a few annoying Germans. The elderly lounge pianist (who looked like Yasser Arafat on Quaaludes) kept playing "Strangers in the Night," so we split. Out in the square after dark, the local musicians were already banging away. The new hygiene craze in Marrakech is so strict that the little capuchin monkeys that amuse tourists now must wear plastic diapers. The air is full of savory smoke from the dozens of grills, and groups of locals and tourists surround performances by street musicians, storytellers, acrobats, salesmen and comedians. We called a swinging band of small guys playing northern hill music "the Jibli Midgets." A competent Gnawa troupe, which played with their backs against their lined-up motor bikes, were "the Gnawa Bikers." A transvestite crew of dancing boys, in makeup and full drag, were so skillfully tarted up that they looked more like girls than girls. For some reason, we called them "the Spice Turtles." They appeared to be doing a thriving business among the foreign tourists.

Wandering in the souks, I bought some Saharan silver earrings for a friend back home. One shop had some very dread-looking nomad knives in their camel-hide sheaths, obviously pre-owned and well used. A container of star-quality crafts and antiques had just come in from Niger, we were told, and the souks were full of sub-Saharan delights and avant-African décor.

Supper was pizza and a tagine on the roof terrace of Les Premicis, overlooking the teeming Jmaa el Fna, now lit by a thousand bulbs. Then an eerie walk home through the darkened, shuttered medina. On the way, Johar bought a quarter kilo of fresh cherries picked that morning in Ouarika, a verdant valley in the nearby mountains, and a half kilo each of inexpensive figs and dates from Iraq. That country's poor farmers are so desperate that their exported produce – grown in the valley of the Tigris and the Euphrates rivers – sells for half the price of locally grown fruit – and tastes better, according to Johar.

Johar programs more of Manu Chao in the salon – that hippy! What does Johar hear in this music that I don't? I washed the city's red dust off in the unlit rooftop shower. The hot water felt silken on my dry skin in the cool evening air. The Koutoubia mosque was a quiet sentinel in the evening darkness. After a few shots of Tamrirt fig liqueur, even Manu Chao sounded groovy.

May 7th.

Three a.m. My fourth night in Marrakech was sleepless. I sat up reading *Ivanhoe* and drinking cold Sidi Ali water, imagining it gushing from sacred springs in the mountains. Open to the night is the dark courtyard and its silent fountain tiled in bottle green. Suddenly the first muezzin begins to chant, followed by the rest, the glottal prayers floating in the ether.

The previous day I lay out in the early morning sun. The Atlas Mountains were still invisible. The pale yellow Saharan light was only bearable in short bursts, with cold showers in between. I made scrambled eggs for the lads, served with toasted rounds of the coarse barley bread that Johar buys. The eggs drew another compliment from

Driss, who is particular about his food. Driss has asked for a raise in salary, plus health benefits for him and his family – which is now supposed to be the law in Morocco, but is often interpreted in different ways. Johar told Driss he would have to think about it. (Hope Driss doesn't kill us.)

It was a hot day, so we mostly chilled. That's the great thing about Marrakech.

In the late afternoon, we walked to the Koutoubia mosque and found a petit taxi to drive us to Gueliz, the European suburb of Marrakech, now booming with chaotic traffic amid the construction sites of new hotels and apartment buildings. Gueliz used to be a sleepy and proudly colonial relic of French empire, but the town is now full of middle class Moroccans, and visitors more accustomed to the amenities of a modern city than to the cramped warren of the medina. (A French woman friend of mine, from a proud *Provençal* Catholic family, married a Turkish architect a few years ago. They moved to Gueliz, where he has more business than he can handle, and she has four sons. They seem to be a typically affluent Gueliz couple of the 21st century.)

I bought some books in the well-stocked, polyglot Libraire Chatr on the main boulevard, and then we inspected some of

Gueliz's upscale boutiques, art galleries and antiquaries. We wanted an early supper at Al Fassia, a chic restaurant run exclusively by women from the northern city of Fez, but it was closed for two weeks. Instead we ate a sizzling pizza, slathered with olive paste and a white, ricotta-like cheese, at the Pizzeria Little Italy, behind the Hotel Diwane on rue Yugoslavie.

The sun began to set behind Mount Gueliz, the immense, jagged rock that looms over the town. A panicked vodka run to the ACIMA supermarket was foiled by the strict 8 p.m. curfew for purchasing alcohol in Marrakech. We arrived at 8:02, but the metal gate was already drawn over the wine department, and the manager was having none of my pleading. "Terminé," he said, with terrible finality. So we grabbed a petit taxi back to the Koutoubia, passing a big McDonald's on the boulevard, with a long queue of young Moroccans waiting to get inside. Then back to the empty bar of Les Jardins de Koutoubia, and the one (or two) vodka and tonics. The hotel is built around a beautiful, quite large swimming pool, a silent mirror of the sky at this time of the evening when most of the guests were at table. We walked around the dark blue expanse, and found an old Gnawa lurking in a shadowy corner, with his 4-stringed sentir silent at his side, and no guests to play for. Once upon a time, Gnawa musicians were looked upon with dread by modernists, much like the Rastafarians were once reviled by polite society in Jamaica. Now, some of the better hotels here have an in-house Gnawa musician to add *ambience* to their 21st century sterility.

Back in the smoking square, we stopped to groove along with the Gnawa Bikers, who were running hot that night. Their iron castanets were banging away, and the lead sentir put out a sonorous, bass-heavy rhythm. There were six of them, with a couple of young dancers out front who were aggressively soliciting contributions from onlookers.

A veiled local woman, and her three daughters, had stopped to listen to the Gnawa. One of the little girls, about eight years old, began to twitch and roll her eyes and move her hips to the African backbeat. When the mother looked down and saw this, she quickly pulled her girls away from the devil music and hurried away.

Walking down the hill, we bought hot barley bread and fresh eggs from the all-night egg man near the 24/7 lamp shop. We passed a recently collapsed house, someone's calamity open to the sky. Lean cats prowled the dusty alleys, ignoring humans except to avoid being run over by speeding motorbikes. At the entry to Derb Sidi Manaraf is a hammam – a public bath house. At night the air is fragrant with burning cedar chips – detritus of nearby carpentries – that heat both the hammam's bathwater and the ovens of the little bakery next door. We listened to the BBC news on the roof, and talked and smoked for the rest of the evening.

The mosque woke me at four o'clock, and I thought about the Gnawa we'd heard earlier in the Jmaa el Fna. Then I accessed a vague memory of my first visit to Marrakech, twenty years earlier. The big square was still an African bus terminal and market place: hot, filthy, and very dusty, with brigades of beggars and troupes of acrobats vying for attention from the few tourists and crowds of peasants in mountain dress. One night I was listening to a Gnawa band with a friend who had lived in Marrakech for twenty years. She said she thought that these were the Gnawas who were playing one evening in 1967 when Brion Gysin brought Brian Jones into the square. The founder of the Rolling Stones became fixated on the smoking gear of the *moqaddem*, or leader, of the Gnawas. The *sebsi* wasn't anything special, but the musician's *mutwi*, his leather kif pouch, was laden with old coins, coral beads, plastic charms, black cat bones, leather amulets, monkey hair, carnelian, jade-like amazonite, and other *joujoux*. As Gysin later told her, Brian Jones went crazy for this paraphernalia, and after a serious haggle Gysin got it off the *moqaddem* for some absurd price.

The Rolling Stones, or at least Mick Jagger, Keith Richards and Brian, had been visiting Marrakech in the wake of highly publicized drug arrests earlier that year. But Brian had been behaving badly in Marrakech. He beat up his famous girlfriend, model Anita Pallenberg, and then went off with some Berber prostitutes whose groins were decorated with intricate, basket-woven tattoos. When Brion Gysin delivered Brian Jones back to the Stones' hotel, they found that Mick and Keith had absconded, with Anita in tow. Brian Jones had lost his friends, his girl, and his band in Marrakech. It was the end of an era.

And here we were, twenty years later – and twenty years ago. My friend wondered if any of these Gnawa had played in the square in 1967. Had any of these guys seen a rich, dissolute hippie in pop star finery bargaining for Uncle Ahmed's *mutwi*? (Which Brian of course lost at London's

Heathrow airport when he tried to bring the reeking object through British customs.)

And this evening: were Uncle Ahmed's grandsons responsible for luring a dark-eyed little Marrakech girl toward the unspeakable mysteries of the Gnawa?

5/7:

Morning very warm. Driss arrives with a paper sack of big Ouarika cherries. They're tartly juicy and go great with Danone vanilla yoghurt. Then eggs mayonnaise on barley toast. After some false starts, I master the French instructions for the combo washer-drier, and suddenly we have clean clothes.

I take some sunrays on the roof, supervised by two cats. The males have all their gonads and strut around like little jaguars. The females dart from roof to roof, sly and shy, silent little spirits. A French neighbor has one of those screaming Pekinese dogs that sounds like a coyote killing a rabbit. My morning reading is the *Times Literary Supplement*, two months behind as usual.

Soon Cherif shows up, and it's time for some business. Johar has to see a colleague on the outskirts, so we pick up Driss's old Peugeot in the Place Moukef and head out, leaving the medina through the

Bab el Khemis gate. This is Driss's first car, but he says he wants to sell it because gas is too expensive. Cherif, annoyingly, keeps giving Driss unwanted driving tips.

The road out of town is bordered on both sides by new construction on a scale that must be unprecedented for modern Africa. Marrakech is exploding into vast suburbs of housing faster than architects and construction firms can keep up. Cherif tells us the price of rebar and concrete had doubled in the past 18 months. We head to the huge Quartier Industriel, and the showrooms and workshop of top Moroccan designer Moulay Nacer. His firm, Bahja Export, manufactures clothes for local and European markets, and his exquisite stock of antiques and furnishings are wholesaled to merchants in the medina who sell them in the souks. He and his family live out here in desert suburbia, but he is currently refurbishing a splendid old medina palace, at mind-boggling expense (whose back door happily opens into the dead end of Derb Sidi Manaraf). Moulay says his kids can't wait for the family to move into the medina, where all the cool people live. The only delay is that his wife's sister has mental issues. She needs looking after, and he's having a special space built to accommodate her.

Moulay is a happening guy with a designer's eye and a perfect command of English, because he toured around the States with an American girlfriend back in the misty Eighties. His smart showrooms look and feel like Harrods, or Bloomingdales, presenting chic furniture and textiles in subtle silken colors. We're served mint tea, and are joined by a friend of Moulay's, who just happened to be there – a man in a suit and tie, someone I immediately took for a police official. This guy wanted to know about the American election, and I told him, with total certainty, that Mr. Obama had no chance of winning the presidency. Johar said he fervently hoped Obama would win. The guy took this all in, and sipped the sugary tea. After awhile, Moulay took me into his workrooms, and I was allowed to buy (for a pittance) some dresses, caftans and shawls for my women back home. The local bank rejected my credit card over the phone, and other arrangements were made.

An hour later, as the sun reclined behind the big mountain, Driss dropped us off in Gueliz, where we visited the ACIMA supermarket and picked up two litres of French vodka ("Donskaia"), ripe avocados, goat cheese, and green bottles of Stork, one of the local beers. A petit taxi took us back to the 'hood, where our passage was delayed by a flock of rams blocking the street, and then again by a brief, but violent, fist fight between two youths outside of a video arcade jammed with kids.

I was now determined to mix a batch of "Nuclear Waste," a toxic cocktail publicly espoused by Keith Richards. Keith's basic recipe is two ounces of vodka topped with Sunkist orange soda, and served on ice. The local version of corporate Sunkist in Morocco is called "Hawai," and it blended quite well with the Donskaia vodka and the (blessedly plentiful) Sidi Ali ice cubes from Johar's freezer. We were enjoying this crass aperitif when Ahmed dropped by with a golf ball of fresh kif, tightly wrapped in plastic.

Some time went by. Shadows moved across the courtyard tiles, and the sky gradually darkened.

Later, we cut through the Souk des Babouches and walked up the glittering rue Semmarine, one of the most glamorous market streets in the world, whose merchants offer almost every beautiful thing available in Morocco, but also crafts and herbs and antiques shipped across the desert from Mali, Niger and Senegal. When we arrived in the Jmaa el Fna, all the food shops were working and wood smoke filled the dusty evening air. Bypassing the long row of snail vendors, we started with lamb sausages, spitting from the grill, but served to us without the customary dish of tomato salsa, which Johar pronounced "risky" from bitter past experience. Despite the sanitized, electrified, and standardized municipal oversight of the open-air kitchens, with licensed cooks identified by plastic laminates hanging from their necks, we are still in Africa, where a pesky microbe can seriously fuck you up.

For the next course, we walked a few yards to the seafood kitchens, and sat down to plates of fried sole fillets, chunks of crispy cod, baby salmon steaks, and delicious grilled squid, all served with piping hot peppers and steaming greens. While I was pontificating on the interesting differences between the British and American pressings of *Aftermath* with Johar, a beggar reached over my shoulder, snatched up my bread, and disappeared into the crowd.

There was a lot of music on offer in the Jmaa el Fna after supper. Some very good rhaita players were blaring loud snake-charming airs. The Gnawa Bikers were banging on their metal castanets and twirling the tassels on their cowry-covered hats. Off to the side, opposite the brightly lit shops of lantern dealers, we noticed a big crowd of

Moroccans gathered around an older singer wearing an immaculate white caftan, a white Berber skullcap, and metal aviator sunglasses. He sang and brayed in a sandpaper voice – an extremely funky apparition accompanied by a banjo and three drummers, and he had the crowd of locals laughing out loud as he performed bawdy routines about farm animals, made fun of yokels in from the mountains for a night on the town, and just sang old songs in a hilarious and evidently very suggestive way. (The young girls in tight jeans seated on benches close to the musicians were red-cheeked from laughing; a few drew the fringes of their headscarves up to their eyes in giggling embarrassment.) The great thing about this classic Marrakech street griot was his young rhythm section. They sang with him on the choruses, and they totally rocked out, deploying the old-fashioned Berber backbeat that owns the listener in two seconds. We listened to him for half an hour, and really dug his comedy act combined with old songs and an absolute command of his appreciative audience, who handed over money to his retainers between songs. This was the best music we'd heard so far in Marrakech, the true soul of this red city, and I resolved to come back for more.

Refreshed by an expensive (ten dirhams) glass of freshly squeezed grapefruit juice from one of the dozen citrus wagons, we looked into an old fondouk near the Bab Fteuh. Once an inn for traders, drovers, and visiting merchants from the south, the fondouk now housed antique shops specializing in nomadic wares, and old, or reproduction, Dogon-style wooden doors from Mali. I was tempted by a funky Tuareg knife, in its original red leather shoulder scabbard. The knife was as keen as a razor, and looked as if it had a bloody history, like a numinous weapon from a Borges tale. I didn't buy it, to my later regret, because when I got back to the shop later, it had been sold.

At the big spice emporium next door, we bought fresh coffee and argan butter, then proceeded down Derb Mouassine, picking up sacks of fresh plums and tangerines from the countryside. By the Mouassine mosque, we passed through a teeming village of music shops and band HQs, where local ensembles can be hired to play for weddings, baby naming parties, or djinn removal from your home. Dodging careening motorbikes and street soccer games, we fell into a Gnawa lair, where some young guys were sitting on a carpet playing cards while an older master in a pale blue *gandura* laid down a soulful bass line on his sentir. The shop had some really nice Gnawa hats for sale, beaded in gleaming white cowry shells. I was tempted.

Out on the street, a giant pair of eyeglasses in blue and orange neon advertised an optometrist. The air was full of household cooking and excited kids. Someone was blasting Um Kalthoum, the Rising Star of the East, from a music stall. Johar bought some almond pastries to have with our tea, and we walked the rest of the way home.

Another round of Nuclear Waste, a few pipes of Ahmed's finest, and Johar was off on the story of sad betrayal by his trusted local manager, Hassan. After years of honest service, Hassan embezzled money from Johar's firm and gambled it away with the connivance of Abdelatif Zanaqi, who then drank battery acid. Johar described a very tense, climactic meeting with Hassan's extended family, at which the shamed miscreant sat, and said not a word, while his relatives pleaded for Hassan's wife to take his place in managing Johar's business in Marrakech. Johar told them he would think about this, but later decided never to have any dealings with this family in the future. "In Morocco, family is everything," he said. "Of course, their first loyalty is to each other. There's nothing wrong with that. But I have my own family to think about."

From a distance, we heard some Gnawa music, and I recalled a Gnawa party we had at Johar's old house in Derb El Hammam – a cozy little place he tried to buy from an old Berber shopkeeper who refused to sell it to him at a fair price. The seven Gnawa musicians had arrived after sunset, and they played their Saharan blues music for two hours, before a huge feast was laid on: soups, tagines, pigeon pies, roasted goat, pastries, mint tea. Many pipes, and hours of music later, the Gnawa chief informed us that the exorcism was almost complete. Only the sacrifice of a young camel stood between us and the final removal of unwelcome djinn from the property. We declined the honor of a sacrifice, and the long night came to an end.

I said good night to Johar, and retired to bed to continue *Ivanhoe*, whose thrilling tale unfolded behind my eyes like a Romantic prose movie. Lord Byron was such a fan of Sir Walter Scott that the lord had his footman wait outside the printer's shop (Byron and Scott shared a publisher, John Murray) to grab the first pages of any new Waverly novel as they came, hot off the press.

May 9.

At two o'clock in the dark morning, a mosquito buzzed in my ear and woke me from a stressful dream about a cocaine deal. I got up and padded down the old house's cold stone steps, and sat in the dark salon for a while, just listening to the quiet night. Soon I returned to sleep.

At four o'clock, the call to prayer began groaning from the Ben Youssef mosque, followed by calls from every minaret in the medina. These devotions shake the city out of its sleep and into the reality of a new day.

At 5:30, clouds drifted over from the north, as the blood-orange sun rose over the desert, followed by thicker clouds and brief rain showers. I spent the day working on a text about Bob Marley's childhood that my agent wanted to sell to a publisher in New York.

A new table was delivered, late in the morning, by Moulay's men. Artfully tiled, supported by iron legs, it was designed for Johar's office, replacing a funky wooden desk that dated from the Banana Tree House. This old table was carried up to my room and became my bookstand.

That afternoon I began to look through some of the books I'd bought in

Gueliz a few days earlier. World-famous Moroccan sociologist Fatima Mernissi's *L'Amour dans les Pays Musulmans* is a reissue, published by Le Fennec in Casablanca, of a study of romantic Islamic literature first published in Paris in 1984. Fatima is the best-known Moroccan intellectual in the world, having authored the classic feminist study *Beyond the Veil* in 1975. I met her when a friend brought her to lunch at my house near Boston when she was in town for medical treatment, circa 1980. My wife made a quiche, and we drank a little white wine with the meal. Then a pipe or two, and I put on a Gnawa record and we grooved the afternoon away. I tried to contact her when I was in Rabat a couple years later, but my calls were not returned.

I put down Fatima's text and then, in the space of two hours, I read a slim and cunning novel, *D'Argile et de feu* by Mohammed-Hounaine El-Hamiani. His theme was the confluence of the "real" world with the spiritual realm of the djinn. The book was published in 2006 by the Rabat firm Editions LPL (La Plume Libre), and El-Hamiani has been hailed as the next Moroccan writer to watch, in the considerable wake of Tahar Ben Jelloun. The title – *Of Clay and Fire,* in my translation – refers to Allah's assertion in the Koran that he created mankind from clay, and that he made the djinn from flames.

Evening, fall of day. We walked, slowly, up the rue Semmarine through throngs of tour groups and local shoppers. The upscale souk had many temptations on offer: stunning contemporary jewelry; Moroccan antique pieces; incredible beaded camel bags from Mali depicting serpents and spiders; fierce looking knives and short swords; old wooden doors from Niger; Tuareg saddles and spears. We stepped into The Golden Door, the most expensive of the antique dealers with an international clientele and lots of museum-quality junk. They have a photo wall of famous visitors, including Mrs. Clinton and her daughter, Paul McCartney and his ex-wife, Posh and Becks, Tom Cruise and Nicole Kidman, and lots of French celebrities like Carla Bruni and Jean-Paul Belmondo.

For some reason, Johar was interested in the fancy three-story pizza restaurant that fronts on the Jmaa el Fna, but I begged off and we ate roasted lamb, dusted with cumin and salt, at one of the outdoor grills. The mint tea served with the lamb was strong and invigorating, so we got up and followed the sound of music. The old Berber comedian was performing in his spot, again surrounded by about a hundred customers, all Moroccan. Tonight he was working with a banjo-drum-tambourine trio, and they were wailing away while he hitched up the hem of his white gondura and shook his bum in a splendidly jive dance which made the whole crowd laugh with him. Then he stopped the music with a wave of his hand and launched into some satiric patter that made the pretty, sloe-eyed Berber girls seated down front giggle with embarrassment. The whole performance – the music, the comedy, the timing – was totally great; people like him have been performing here for centuries. When his assistant passed the hat, I threw in all the dirhams I had.

The show stopped at nine o'clock, and the musicians' place was taken over by sellers of folk medicines, love potions and herbal remedies for "erectile dysfunction." Selling space in the Jmaa el Fna is now carefully monitored by the city, with every specialty from snake charmers to snail sellers allotted specific times at certain areas. As the crowd dispersed, Johar led the way toward the Mellah, the old Jewish ghetto of Marrakech. At one time Jewish families held a monopoly over the salt trade, and "mellah" is the word for salt in Darija, the national dialect. Early European visitors noted that the severed heads of the sultan's enemies were brought to the Mellah to be salted for preservation and ultimate exhibition in the square. As we moved along the dusty streets, past the occasional no-star backpacker hotels, I noticed the little iron balconies hanging over the street, in sharp contrast to the faceless walls of the medina. Johar remarked that when the Mellah was thriving, Jewish women allowed themselves to be seen on their balconies, part of the lively street scene forbidden to their Moslem sisters, who socialized only on their rooftops. Today the Mellah is a poverty area, distinguished by a large (and once kosher) market, a street of gold merchants, a few upscale lounges in the old houses, and a jazz club in a restored riad. In the middle of this are the ruins of the Badia palace, a millennium old, and the vast Palais Bahia, the Marrakech residence of Thami El Glaoui, legendary Lord of the Atlas and Pasha of Marrakech. Tonight the palace was locked down and guarded by armed police, as if the old warlord, who received Churchill and Franklin Roosevelt here during the war, was still in command.

    Back in Derb Sidi Manaraf, we chatted with the smiling guardian who was on duty until one o'clock. The neighbors are always glad when Johar visits his house because they are guaranteed a decent night's sleep. The guardian urgently whispers to Johar that his sister is an expert housekeeper and looking for work, but Johar is already paying Driss to look after the house and politely declines.

By itself, the French vodka tastes like white lightning; but mixed with Hawai orange soda, the Donskaia takes on an appealing flavor of clove-tinged Sterno. The rest of the evening is spent in the softly lit library, recently hung with beautiful new prints of photographs that Johar made in the mountains up north. Our old Jajouka friends looked down on us while we filled pipes and I listened to epic accounts of Johar's adventures in Ibiza (where he ran a leather shop), Majorca (where he dated Robert Graves' god-daughter), Jajouka (where he recorded one of the tribe's better discs), and Tangier (where he began his short career as a smuggler by secreting two hundred pounds of primo hashish from the Rif into the welded-shut frame of a vintage Land Rover and shipping it into the port of Baltimore, back in the misty Sixties.) I went to bed at midnight, with the door and iron-grated window open to the evening breeze. At three in the morning, a chilling damp mist fell over the medina, and I stayed awake for an hour, acutely aware of the stillness of the night.

May 10.

In the morning we walked up to the Jmaa el Fna for steaming bowls of *bisar*, the thick fava bean soup that is a breakfast staple all over Morocco. Around us the mutton cooks were stuffing great chunks of lamb into the underground roasting pits, where the heavily spiced meat would bake all day and be ready for the evening meal. Johar then tagged along when I plunged into the souks. First stop was Al Yed ("The Eye"), a Berber jewelry shop owned by an old friend of Johar's, Mustapha Ouizid. When he was younger, Mustapha was just another dealer in silver finery, old wedding stuff and occasional Judaica. Now he styles himself an *antiquaire*, and his prices have risen accordingly. His Derb Mouassine shop, a hangout for foreigners living in the medina, is full of coin silver, blue turquoise, red coral, old yellow amber, toffee-colored carnelian, jade green amazonite, jet-black jet. He asks us about the American election, says he hates Bush ("Boosha"), and overcharges me for two pairs of earrings. As we leave the shop, a street fight breaks out in Fhal Chidmi, the little square outside.

Voices are raised and fists fly for about ten seconds before the two young combatants are separated amid angry reproaches for scaring away the tourists upon whom the shopkeepers depend.

A few steps away, we ducked into Art Akhnif, a rug store, where we were given mint tea and shown about two hundred flat-woven *hambl* pillows, all decorated with geometric patterns and mysterious glyphs and symbols which, someone in Tangier once assured me, represented the only survival of the lost alphabet of Atlantis. I bought a bunch of these, and then headed to the textile souk for some scarves woven in the new style called *sabra*, made from locally produced silk and dyed in wonderful muted colors. The last stop was the spice market, for knitted cotton Berber caps, all colorful and tempting to the eye.

Our evening meal, at home, was toasted barley bread with avocado and fresh goat cheese, bought on the street and wrapped in green leaves, washed down with cold Stork beer and chilled green melon. After a pipe or two and the news on the radio, I began to get chills and body aches. I cursed the ill luck of this. Having once contracted a case of hepatitis up north, thirty years ago, I knew from sad experience that

Morocco is no place to be ill. A night of *tourista* – sweat, cramps and the runs – ensued, ameliorated by liberal doses of blessed Pepto-Bismol, and mercifully I felt better by the dawn call to prayer.

Saturday May 11th.

As Abdullah was filling his sebsi with fresh kif, the first pipe of our day, he noticed pictures of Barak Obama and John McCain on the front page of the previous day's *Paris Herald Tribune* (as I still think of the thin little newspaper, this edition printed in Madrid, that gets to Morocco a day late). He asked me which I preferred in the coming American election, and I explained that I hated them both, indeed that I hated all politicians. This made Ahmed laugh and engendered an epic coughing fit. I didn't mention that I rarely vote, because it only encourages the politicians.

Up on the roof, an astounding sight: the first crystal-clear morning of this visit revealed the full grandeur of the awesome Atlas Mountains that loom over Marrakech to the south. The peaks are snow-capped and gleaming in the desert air, a thrilling vista not always visible to those who come here for a brief stay. The tallest, Jbel Toubqal, is thought to be the highest peak in North Africa. All one can do is stand there in awe.

Interested in breakfast, Johar and I strolled back up to the *bisar* kitchen and ordered bowls of the thick porridge, each served with a ladle of dark olive oil and rounds of wheaten bread. My antique Swatch had stopped after twenty years – typical timeless Marrakech – and I visited a watch repair shop facing the square, but the replacement battery didn't work either and that was the end of it. When I turned around, a boy held a cobra up to my face, and laughed when I realized it was cunningly made of wood and plastic. A toy vendor was selling a hilarious mechanical game depicting a hapless George W. Bush chasing grinning Osama Bin Ladin around a little metal platform. A man in a jellaba walked by with a pair of diapered capuchin monkeys on short leads.

Then, on the way to buy the newspapers, we came across the Berber singer/comedian/storyteller whose act we'd been enjoying almost nightly for several days. He was alone, sitting on a bench in his usual spot in front of the lantern souk, as if holding his place and waiting for the sun to go down. We shook his hand and asked his name. Abdelhakim, he told us. He had been performing in this spot for many years, he said, and produced from his briefcase a sheaf of laminated magazine stories about him in Italian and Spanish. I told him how much we enjoyed his music and asked if he would pose for a photo with me. He was very agreeable, and sold us two copies of his CD, which, he explained, is only available during the day because he's too busy working at night to keep track of sales. As the disc had no writing on it, I asked its title. "*Jmaa el Fna,*" he replied. "I'm here every night, from six o'clock to nine," he reminded us. We said we would return for the evening performance. Two girls on a motorbike almost swerved into us, missing by inches. Ten minutes later, in a crowded lane, a donkey cart laden with construction debris rolled over the edge of my shoe.

The afternoon was very hot, and I repaired to Johar's elegant but rarely used salon for a siesta. The main room of the house was dark, and relatively cool. I slept through two hours of lingering microbial disturbance.

After a refreshing shower on the roof, watched by a silent male alley cat with big pendulous balls, I listened to the BBC radio news and sat with Johar in his office while he completed some paperwork. I also took up another of the books I'd bought in Gueliz: *Marrakesh: Through Writers' Eyes*.

This British publication is an anthology of historical and travel writing about this city, starting with ancient exploration accounts, progressing through the early modern era (Capt. John Smith!) and the Enlightenment, and continuing into colonialism and the 20th century. The writers include Elias Canetti, Juan Goytisolo (a current resident of Le Rouge, perhaps its most famous); Edith Wharton, Leo Africanus, George Orwell, Gavin Maxwell (author of *Lord of the Atlas,* the classic biography of Thami El Glaoui); Esther Freud (*Hideous Kinky*), and Christopher Gibbs, the London antiques dealer who was famously busted with the Rolling Stones in 1967, and who has been a longtime resident of both the hills above Tangier and those above Marrakech. For the rest of my stay, Johar and I poured over this indispensable book, gleaning much crucial information.

A potted history of Marrakech would start a thousand years ago, when this place was a well-watered oasis of olives, fruit and palms. In the eleventh century a horde of jihad warriors – the Al-Murabitun (Almoravid in French) – swarmed over the mountains from the south, imposing a more puritanical Islam born in the wastes of the Western Sahara. They occupied the valley and called it Marrakech – which means roughly "Cross and Hide." After establishing a large military camp, the Murabitun armies went north, conquering Berber kingdoms as they raged over the land. This was the beginning of the Moroccan empire that eventually ruled much of Spain and northwest Africa. One of their leaders, Youssef ibn Tachfine, is credited with founding Morocco City, as it was known on the early maps. His tomb, a modest affair near the Jmaa el Fna, is the only survivor of the Murabitun, since another wave of holy warriors crossed the mountains a few generations later and wiped out almost every trace of them.

We again took our supper at Chez Chegrouni by the crowded square, now bathed in soft evening light. Over very hot plates of couscous, chicken and lamb, Johar told me the sad story of our old friend Pillhead's last visit to Marrakech. Pillhead was my nickname for a friend and client of Johar's, an intrepid Sixties veteran of the Afghan hippie trails, who made several trips to Morocco in the 1990s to buy stock for his décor emporium in Los Angeles. (I dubbed him Pillhead because of his aggressive fondness for the Xanax tranquilizers in my medicine kit.)

This raw-boned son of the American southwest liked to raise a little hell now and then, and he would get bored sitting around at night like Johar and me, just smoking and talking and listening to music. One night in (maybe) 2003, he and his brother went out on a spree and ended up at the Hotel Marrakech, which has a nightclub whose main attractions are young Moroccan girls, in not many clothes, eager to sell themselves to foreigners like Pillhead and his bro – who ended up, extremely intoxicated, with two young Berber girls (complete with tattoos). They checked into the hotel for the night, paying with Pillhead's credit card. A month later in West Hollywood, Mrs. Pillhead opened the Amex statement to discover that the hotel had charged her husband ten thousand dollars for his night of moral turpitude in the presidential suite. Pillhead tried to protest, but the hotel produced a signed card receipt and refused to budge. "The wages of sin," Johar said, shaking his head and trying not to laugh.

We spent the rest of the evening grooving to Abdelhakim's hard rocking CD, a seriously percussive masterpiece of south Moroccan street music recorded both in the square and in a proper recording studio. (Die, Manu Chao!) I'm playing the scaly thing as I type these words, and my toes are tapping and my hips are twisting, involuntarily, in my chair.

11 May

Storks flapping on the roof woke me early, and I climbed softly up the stone steps to try to get a close look at them. They'd flown off by the time I got up there, leaving nothing but the dazzling sun reflected off the snowcaps of the mountains overhead. I went down, made coffee, sat in a straw chair in the shade of the salmon-colored courtyard, and read a long review of a biography of Rudolf Nureyev in the *Times Literary Supplement*, several old issues of which I had carried with me from Boston in a futile attempt to catch up to the current one. When Johar woke up, he drank some coffee and smoked a pipe, and kindly asked if I wanted to drive to Essaouira for a meal of grilled seafood on the quays. This is one of the great pleasures of the southern Moroccan coast, and then one can roam the old Portuguese ramparts and buy exquisite objects made from local fruitwood. But we'd done this on my last visit, and I was happy to feel "deep medina" on this one. The following month in June, Essaouira would host its annual Gnawa festival, when all the best hoodoo groups from "Soudaniya" vie for best in show. This is a 24/7 marathon of musical djinnappeasement, and the old port town vibrates with drums and iron clappers all day and night. ("You smoke stoned," a young Gnawa had told me some years before. "Then music very good!) The idea and sensory anticipation of fresh langoustes – drenched in lemon and pepper and sizzling on a brazier next to the boat that brought it in – was appealing, but I told Johar I wanted to stay in Marrakech, and just groove. Mogador: next time. (Insha'Allah.)

Late in the morning we emerged from shadowy Derb Sidi Manaraf into the blinding light of the open street. Young men were washing themselves by a fountain in the wall of the hammam. Music was in the air as a Gnawa in designer shades and a cowry-shell cap sat on a worn carpet in the street and played a bass line on his sentir against the ochre wall. His yellow slippers and a tea tray were at his side. Bicycle bells tinkled and motorbike horns squawked as the stream of humanity, machines and donkey carts moved up the hill. Johar wanted some olives, so we ducked into the covered souk that deals in wholesale spices and preserves. Each shop offered huge basins of olives of every size, color, taste, and description. The air was pungent with brine. Besides olives, the stalls featured preserved lemons stacked high in two-liter jars, and all sort of pickled peppers and fruit. A crocodile of Russian tourists wielding cell phone cameras clicked and flashed around us, as Johar bought meaty, maroon-colored olives and big green capers, packed in their juices. Then we detoured for a few rounds of the barley bread he favored – a real peasant bread, that – and then headed back for lunch through Les Teinturies, the famous dyer's souk with acres of Technicolor cloth drying in the afternoon sun. Different dyes are used on different days, and today the major color was the dark red of Tibetan monk robes, giving the entire souk the atmosphere of a misty mountain kingdom.

At the foot of Souk Talaa, my attention was diverted by some oil paintings in the La Qoubba Gallery, opposite the Museum of Marrakech. While worshippers spilled out the rear door of the Ben Youssef mosque during noon prayers, prostrating themselves in the dusty street, we checked out a series of big oils depicting relaxed kif smokers, lush Atlas landscapes, and gay laundry hanging in the medina. I was intrigued by some new work by the popular Marrakech street/graffiti artist who calls himself Ouida, and was able to bargain a small watercolor of his fiery calligraffiti down to a hundred dollars.

We found a giant ripe avocado in the refrigerator, and couldn't remember buying it, but we cut it in half and filled it with soft goat cheese and sliced boiled egg and a little olive oil. This was washed down with sparkling Oulmes water on ice, and finished with cold green melon slices. After the siesta, the ever-jolly Abdelkrim "Busta" appeared, our old friend of twenty years who makes belts for Johar's company. Busta had two new belts for me, both with large chunks of turquoise set in the crosshatched metal buckles. This blue stuff had been bought by Johar at the famous Tucson Gem Show, and hand-carried by him into Morocco, and not without considerable duty paid at the airport. (Demand for semi-precious stones is now so high in Morocco that they are scarce and very expensive. Likewise, once abundant red coral beads – traditionally worn by Berber brides to inspire fertility – now are most likely imported from India.)

Busta is a solid, burly guy with a wide smile and a big family. He's one of the premier leather artisans in Marrakech, and that's saying something. He doesn't smoke with us, but he's laughing all the time anyway. I've brought some snapshots of my family, house, pets, garden and so on. He looks at each once intently, then brings out his own family snaps from his wallet – one for each of his six kids and one of his veiled wife. The eldest girl is studying at the nursing college in Fez. I remark that family life is very expensive, and Busta nods sadly. I pour him a cold Hawai over ice cubes, because it's too hot for tea.

The call to prayer came at seven o'clock, as the sun slipped behind the mountains, etching the brown peaks in shadowy relief. On the roof, the Koutoubia minaret loomed between giant palms clacking in the breeze. From a long way off came the crazy bagpipe sound of a rhaita band and drummers. Every house has a satellite dish except this one.

12 mai.

A fresh wind from the north has blown away the city's red dust, and the sky is cobalt blue. We picked up yesterday's newspapers from the kiosk near the Jmaa el Fna and delved into a neighborhood of fondouks, traditional hostels for the traders who pass in and out of Marrakech with everything from spices to amulets to fresh produce. In olden times they stabled their pack animals on the ground floor and slept upstairs. Now, for a few dirhams, the traders can sleep on reed mats, drink tea with other merchants, and a savory tagine is almost always in some state of preparation on a gas fire. Some of the fondouks are also retail outlets for merchandise. Johar and I visited one with a series of second floor shops reached by a steep staircase, pitch-black even at noon. Johar bought a small carved wooden door from Benin, a genuine antique according to the old Berber who managed the shops. I paid a few dirhams for an old wedding fibula, a chained clasp that holds a bride's white robes around her. A fancy fibula is made of coin silver, red coral and semi-precious stones like rubies, or more usually garnets. My fibula is more working class: nickel instead of silver, plastic instead of coral, and red glass in place of gems, but it has the feel of being well used and sold only out of death or desperation.

The metal workshops are only a few yards down the street, and I wanted to visit an artisan from whom I'd bought some mythic Islamic angels, worked in gleaming brass, on my last visit. He might have remembered me as I was walking down the lane amid the tapping of a hundred hammers and the smell of heated metal. He called out "Amerikani!" and held out his hand. He and his colleague were making small hamsas – hands of Fatima – out of shiny white aluminum. I bought a few hands for gifts and declined the artisan's kind offer of mint tea and a sebsi. Back at Derb Sidi Manaraf, Johar matched his new old African door to the alcove harboring the electric fuse box, and was happy to see the fit was perfect.

The north wind cooled the city somewhat, and I spent the afternoon on the roof, idly reading the old copy of *A Life Full of Holes* that I'd borrowed from Johar's extensive shelf of books about Morocco. Paul Bowles tape-recorded his houseboy Larbi Layachi's true tales of grinding poverty in the Rif and hustling in the Tangier of the 1950s. Paul shaped the transcriptions into a text that was first published – as a novel – by Grove Press in 1964. Before the book appeared, Larbi had second thoughts about seeming to be a social critic in a police state, and Bowles arranged for publication under the false name Driss ben Hamid Charhadi. The book was a success in America and England, and the tiny bit of money it earned even allowed the astonished Larbi to look for a bride. But when the French edition was on the press, Larbi got really scared. So Bowles arranged a visa for him, and paid for Larbi to board the steamship *Independence* with Bill Burroughs and sail for New York. Larbi never returned to Morocco. Instead he made a life for himself in California; took English courses at San Francisco State; and (most wonderfully) produced two more books under his own name. The first, *Yesterday and Today*, was published in 1985 by Black Sparrow Press. Dedicated to the memory of Jane Bowles, the text amounts in part to an acute (and very rare) "native" perspective on Paul Bowles and his Tangier expat milieu of the early Sixties. *The Jealous Lover* (Tombouctou Books, 1986) was an unsparing depiction of the poverty and deprivation Larbi endured as a child in postwar Tangier. After that, Larbi disappeared. Some say he lives still. Most likely, he does not.

When the glare of the African sun made the pages of his book too bright to read, I lay back and watched the stratospheric winds sweep high thin clouds and the contrails of jet planes across the sky. I smoked a pipe or two, and drifted off on a pillow-covered couch under the shelter of the rooftop ramada. When I woke, two grey cats sat close by like little leopards, watching me intently. Evidently, I was in their siesta spot, and they seemed annoyed. When I entered the covered staircase to descend, my sun-struck eyes failed in the darkness and I almost pitched down the steep flight of stone steps. I mentioned this to my host, and suggested he install a grab-bar by the light switch. To this suggestion he was congenially agreeable.

That evening, in deep gratitude for his generous hospitality, I invited Johar out for a proper meal at a proper restaurant. A few years ago, there were hardly any restaurants in the medina, and those that did exist featured cliché-classics (couscous, pigeon pie), costumed waiters, and vulgarities like belly dancers. Of course this is changing like everything else. One of the best new restaurants, Le Foundouk, happens to be right around the corner, in a converted fondouk on rue de Souk des Fassi. Arriving at seven o'clock, we had "no reservations," and the place was packed with a youngish clientele on both the ground floor and the balconied second storey. But the chic, black-eyed young hostess led us up to the roof terrace with a few empty tables and a twilight view of the city. It was still very windy, so we took a table in a somewhat sheltered corner, and ordered a bottle of local Semillant Blanc. Gradually the other tables filled with well-heeled Europeans, the women huddling in hats and long scarves against the wind. The menu was French with Moroccan flavors. Soon we were tucking into dishes of filo-wrapped avocados and a delicious lamb *croustillant*, a crunchy meat pie. The Moroccan white wine was cold and tasted like crisp fruit and as dry as a breeze at the beach. Then came a seafood *pastilla*, a fish pie in a crème sauce, and a "tagine Berbère agneau" – lamb goulash served over couscous.

The coffee was very good. The bill was as big as in Paris or New York.

We made our way downstairs, squeezing past harried waiters juggling trays of hot food. As we left, Johar told the hostess that he lived in the neighborhood, and she made him promise to return soon.

Across the street from Le Foundouk was a real, working fondouk, whose ground floor was a carpenter's shop. Johar knew the owner, who was busy building a chair even at this late hour, under a bare bulb. The grubby workshop smelled of sewage, cedar and sawdust, and it was a relief to see that the dreaded gentrification of the medina remains safely in the future (if at all). Back at the house, Johar put on Abdelhakim's hard rockin' CD; I mixed a violent batch of Nuclear Waste, and the remainder of the evening passed into the still of the night.

13/ V

A fine grey mist hung over Marrakech the following morning. The rooftop shower requires discretion and a bathing suit, lest neighbors be offended. But the needles of hot water feel good on my skin, which is beginning to dry out in the desert atmosphere. Throughout the day I keep a pitcher of Oulmes water on ice, and try to stay hydrated.

Johar had business meetings all day. I stayed upstairs to read and write in my darkened room. At four o'clock we walked through streets crowded with children returning home from school, laughing and running with their backpacks, the younger ones hand-in-hand with older brothers and sisters. Our destination was Ahmed's atelier, in a ramshackle district of busy workshops and tiny factories. Here they make a lot of the swag and ornamentation that adorns both traditional and modern Moroccan décor. Ahmed manufactures the metalwork designed by Johar, inspired by Johar's love of Berber zigzag, which are then joined to the intricately crafted leather belts made by Abdelkrim Busta. Johar also designs beautiful handbags, which are cut and sewn by Busta and decorated with hand-crafted medallions – sometimes inlaid with polished cow bone – made by Ahmed. The finished goods are then air-freighted to America and sold in the upscale, rodeo-oriented southwestern American marketplace.

Ahmed received us with his usual grizzled smile, and tiny glasses of hot mint tea. From the folds of his jellaba, he produced a foil-wrapped ball of fresh kif, for which I handed over a few dirhams, with many thanks. As the tapping of hammers, the buzzing of saws, and the whirring of lathes produced a light-industrial din around us, we passed a half hour of serenity amid serious artisanal labor and toil.

I was pretty buzzed – actually seriously intoxicated – when we made our way out of the twisting maze of workshop alleys. The fresh cannabis in the kif is boosted by the strong black tobacco in the mixture, and this stuff of Ahmed's was fucking … was like fucking … *rocket fuel*. The remainder of the day is only a half-experienced blur of color, sensation, … and shameful wackness.

Late in the afternoon, on our way to a hardware store, we passed by the huge Bahia palace, which was about to close to tourists for the day. Seeing it was empty, I paid our way in, and we walked alone down the long forecourt, where Thami El Glaoui had received Roosevelt and Churchill during the last world war. The American president and the British prime minister had attended a conference in Casablanca, and Churchill had insisted – no, *demanded* – that

Roosevelt accompany him to Marrakech to see the sun set behind the high Atlas. His military guard carried Roosevelt (in his wheelchair) up to the high tower of the Villa Taylor, in the palm gardens outside of town, and Churchill's wish was fulfilled.

The Bahia palace sits on two acres of gardens. It was built in the 1880s by a vizier who had started humbly and achieved great wealth and power. He brought the best artisans down from Fez and bade them re-create arabesque architecture and décor to rival the Alhambra in Granada. The result was a kitsch pastiche in its baroque orientalism; was considered vulgar and nouveau-riche by contemporaries; and was handed over in 1912 to the French colonial authority that had taken over the Moroccan sultanate. For some years the palace was a headquarters for General Lyautey, who ran French Morocco for a generation.

The Bahia is still an amazing site, especially the immense harem for the vizier's concubines, consisting of 24 cubicles surrounding a big fountain with an adjacent garden full of bananas, citrus and succulents. The tranquility of the harem, with birds swirling overhead and nesting in the eaves of the colonnade, was far removed from the gritty heat of the town outside. The quiet scene was marred only by two ugly

Spanish couples jabbering to each other in doltish, provincial accents. So we retraced our route through the massive empty rooms of the palace, and proceeded on our errand.

It was six o'clock in the evening now, and the streets were full of red dust and people dodging cars, busses, bikes, mopeds, scooters. The hardware store had beautiful Islamic door knockers, locally made, and the wrought-iron grab-bars that Johar bought so as to avoid discovering my lifeless body at the foot of his staircase. We proceeded down the Riad Zitoun Lakdim, now a pedestrian mall for banks, spas and watch shops, and took over a corner table at the Café Atlas on the south side of the Jmaa el Fna as the vivid orange sun was setting in a fireball. Johar ordered two of the clever Oreo-like coffees where a line of steamed milk appears between two layers of espresso. I sat back and marveled at how totally schwacked I was, hours later, from a few draws of fresh kif earlier in the afternoon.

Then something funny happened. A car stopped a few yards from the café, and a bunch of jazzy-looking Euro hipsters got out and retrieved guitar cases from the boot. The leader was a tall, grey-haired man dressed in black. I immediately realized I knew this person, but could not remember who it was. In fact, I was still so affected by Ahmed's paralytic kif that I only managed to stammer to Joel: "See that guy? He's famous – I think. Or ... something. What? Never mind. I'm so out of it. I need more coffee. Waiter!"

These Paris-looking musicians headed toward an old house we had checked out a few nights before, which was now a nightclub that featured jazz. They must be the band, I thought. Then several horse-drawn buggies rolled past our table, and I noticed that the undercarriages supported cloth bags to catch the equine waste. Monkeys in diapers! Marrakech was taking this hygiene program seriously.

(Two weeks later, I discovered that the tall French musician in the square that evening had been my friend Philip Dalecky, who had befriended and hung out with his girlfriend's tenant, Jim Morrison, in the months before Jim died in Paris in 1971. I had interviewed Philip for my biography of Jim, and had spent subsequent time with him in Paris. But I'd been too stoned to recognize him, out of context, in North Africa – two years after last seeing him.)

When I was able to walk again, we adjourned to a nearby soup kitchen for bowls of steaming barley pearls. This was followed by grilled crevettes from the nearby seafood stalls. The sizzling pink shrimp were served on skewers with harissa and rounds of bread; this made for delicious sandwiches, washed down with mint tea and glasses of Sidi Ali. (The side dishes of greens and fries were greasy and cold, a reminder that it is still possible to find unpleasant food anywhere.)

I turned in early, still gloriously "kifed" (as Brion Gysin used to say), and hoping to wake up the next morning, like everyone else.

Tuesday.

And so my kif holiday continued, bright and early, with fresh coffee and long narrow pipes streaming with diaphanous nymphs of blue smoke. "A pipe of kif before breakfast gives a man the strength of a hundred camels in the courtyard" was an old folk saying amplified by Paul Bowles. He deployed this "Nachaioui Proverb" for the epigraph to *A Hundred Camels in the Courtyard*, the legendary collection of kif tales published in 1962, which made Bowles a folk hero to a generation of hippies that understood the value of this wisdom, and the future it portended.

Driss arrived, as he did every morning, in his long grey robe. He changed into his house clothes in the ground floor storage area where he also laid out his mat and prayed, next to the bicycles and cleaning supplies. Driss used to have a cigarette with us, but his current religiosity forbids this. He washes down the courtyard almost every day, lest the red dust accumulate. Every day he gives me a new Darija word to memorize, in a vain attempt to improve my halting patois of the local speech. He's a good man, so I try to gently encourage Johar to grant him the health benefits he seeks.

Then we're off to the spice market, a smaller version of the town square. A quadrangle of spice stalls, herbalists, small bazaars and notions shops surrounds an acre of crafts vendors selling tourist stuff and Berber caps in wool and cotton. These are knitted by men, and sold in the open market by heavily veiled women protected from the sun by big beach umbrellas. In the morning, these ladies unpack their colorful stock and stack them up for sale, a laborious daily process that we grew fond of watching from the recently opened Café Rahba Lakdima. This French-owned hangout in an old spice house has cool music and attractive staff, and it's packed with foreigners from noon until late. In the early mornings, over *café au lait* and plates of crispy hot crepes served with honey, we witnessed several bitter squabbles among the Berber woman as they quarreled with interlopers trying to set up their wares in the crowded market, where every inch of selling space was already claimed and evidently had been for ages.

Forget trying to cash a traveler's check in a bank branch in the medina of Marrakech unless you have a friend with an account there, and the friend has very friendly relations with the manager.

I saw these huge pink coral beads for sale in an old fondouk. I gaped at them in wonder – "like a hog starin' at a wristwatch," as they used to say in Arkansas. Were they real? The merchant swore they were. I didn't buy them.

I did buy two sebsis and six *sqofa* (pl. of *squf*), the little clay bowls into which one happily inserts the kif. I stumbled across these in the rue Semmarine, to the mild amazement of Johar, who mentioned that kif paraphernalia wasn't much sold in public anymore in Marrakech. Further up the hill, Johar bought a large paper sack of chopped, pit-roasted lamb, which we took home to eat for lunch with coarse, oven-warm barley bread.

Afternoon was a long siesta for me. Many visitors came and went on business with Johar. Moulay's men came to measure the roof for a canvas pavilion. This was supposed to be installed before our arrival, but no. Busta came by, and we drank some Hawai on the rocks, and took some photographs with our arms around each other.

The *International Herald Tribune* was better when Mike Zwerin, the great jazz writer (and musician who played with Miles Davis), was reviewing the European music scene. The thin paper costs 22 dirhams and comes a day late, but as a newspaper junky I'm still eager to grab my copy before the kiosk in the Jmaa el Fna sells out.

Late afternoon on the roof: gray tabby cat sleeps in a shaded corner. A local French language pop station, Radio Douzaine, plays all the hits – planetary and local. Cold shower evaporates on baking skin. French vodka and Hawai orange soda.

Guacamole a la Medina:

4 mashed avocados from Mogador;
2 tbls. Dijon mayonnaise;
2 tbls. fresh *harissa*;
2 tbls. finely chopped red onion;
1 tbls. Worcestershire (or HP) sauce;
Lemon juice, sea salt and black pepper to taste;
Serve with toasted remnants of that morning's baguette, and die happy.

Seven o'clock in the evening. Flocks of swallows whirl over the house, feeding on flying insects. Excited children scream over a heated game of soccer in the street. Two cats take over the roof, fighting or mating or both. My annoyed wife calls and wants to know when I'm coming home. A military band is playing somewhere close by. The wind comes up and doors are shut. The city is blue-gray and quiet.

May 15th.

Another morning of coffee and crepes at the Café Rahba Lakdima, watching the spice market come back to life. The Berber cap sellers stack their wares and call to each other like veiled crows. Carpets are aired out on rooftops across the plaza. Children ride on the backs of bikes and scooters, on their way to school. The sun is already hot at ten o'clock. Skanky-looking European chicks displaying lots of bare skin saunter by, oblivious to local customs and preferences. We decide to split. Johar wants to check out the other establishment run by the people who started this café, so we walk five minutes and visit Terrace, an elegant café/restaurant located on the roof of a renovated gallery of smart shops in Souk Cherifia. The place is empty in the late morning, but is said to be jumping by night. Each seat has a handsome flat-woven pillow for the comfort of guests, who are served on low tables, some in semi-private cubicles. Johar once built and ran a Moroccan restaurant in Arizona, and has a fine eye for what is décor and what is *de trop*. We agreed that this place was ultra-cool if nothing else.

It costs ten dirhams to gain admission to the Musée de Marrakech, the city's largest art museum, just behind Johar's house. A restored caliphal palace, whose massive courtyard is now covered by a tent-like structure, the museum exhibits one of the finest collections of traditional, modern and contemporary arts in Morocco. The undisputed current art star in Morocco is Farid Belkahia, whose symbolist paintings, often adorned with stark Berber imagery, are in many public and private collections in Europe. Roaming around the galleries, I found an atypically lyrical portrait of a girl by our old Tangier nemesis, Mohammed Hamri. I never bought the idea that Hamri was "the painter of Morocco," as he styled himself. But this watercolor was a soft and pretty wash of blues and greens, and made me realize how great it would be to own something painted by the old devil.

I had told my friend Busta that I was leaving the following day, and he was waiting for us when we returned to Derb Sidi Monaraf. He handed me a package wrapped in newsprint. It was a farewell gift of a beautiful mirror, framed in a Moorish arch made of henna-dyed bone. I was very moved by this, and told him that it meant a lot to me to have a long term friendship with a master artisan and excellent man like himself. "Allah atic saha," he said with a smile. "God give you health." We hugged before he left, and Busta told me not to wait another seven years until my next visit.

We dined again on the roof terrace of Le Foundouk, this time in still twilight. The setting sun glinted gold on the three gilded balls atop the Koutoubia minaret. We talked of Paul Bowles, and of our visits with him on various journeys to Tangier. Even the anticipation of those visits was thrilling, a connection with someone who knew expatriate Paris in the Twenties; traveled and studied musical composition amid the radicalism of the Thirties; worked in the New York vanguard of the Forties; inspired the beatniks of the Fifties and the Sixties hippies (*A Hundred Camels in the Courtyard* and Bowles' translation of Mohammed Mrabet's *M'Hashish* were both head shop must-reads); encouraged

Minimalism among composers of the Seventies and provoked hero worship among the rock stars who paid tribute to him in the Eighties. When Paul let you into his dark flat on the third floor of an ugly concrete bunker on the outskirts of town, you entered a shadowy world of hip expatriation, with wood crackling in the fireplace and birds chirping on the plant-shrouded balcony. Paul lay back on a hard sofa, leaning against an intricate, flat-woven Berber tapestry. He chatted with the evening's guests, emptied the tobacco out of filtered cigarettes, re-packed them with the kif that his friend Mrabet chopped and blended for him, fresh every day, and languidly smoked. There was always Ceylon tea served with lemon wedges in very proper china cups and saucers. Sometimes Paul could be catty and provocative, but he was always hospitable and always inspiring. When you left him – maybe he had signed one of his books that you'd bought from the Librairie des Colonnes on the Boulevard Pasteur – you felt like you had interviewed one of the great cultural heroes of the twentieth century. It was a real buzz.

Johar pointed out that Bowles seemed less than smitten by Marrakech. There is barely a mention of the city in his 1972 memoir, *Without Stopping*. When

Bowles had arrived in the Jmaa el Fna in 1961, with Allen Ginsberg in tow, the souks had caught fire and many were destroyed. I said I thought that there must have been something in the hermetic, conspiratorial atmosphere of Tangier that Bowles preferred to the more relaxed life here in the desert.

Back at Le Foundouk, the rooftop terrace was calm and rosy with waning daylight. We dined on very good "surf 'n' turf" – *saumon à la vapeur* and *filet de boeuf* – with a half bottle of Semillant. Afterward, we walked a bit in the quarter, brushed by motorbikes and buffeted by soccer balls. The air was fragrant with cedar smoke from the fire that that heated the corner hammam. I packed my bags and thanked Johar for his kind hospitality, and for two weeks of zero stress. We have been friends since our first voyages to Jajouka in the Jebala hills in 1973, and his love of Morocco continues to inspire me as much, if not more, than even Paul Bowles'. Suddenly I found myself looking forward to my next visit even before the completion of this one. This must have been the feeling Paul once had. Instead of going home, he stayed for the rest of his life.

I was ready for the driver when he walked down the alley at 4:30 the next morning. He humped my suitcase to where his Benz taxi was parked. The car started on the sixth try, and he backed out of the medina at top speed and whip-lashed me to the airport as dawn was breaking, along obscure back roads amid gigantic construction projects. Marrakech and its surroundings will be much changed the next time I'm able to make my way here.

The Royal Air Inter shuttle flight to Casablanca was at 6:15. Then there was a three-hour layover in the new terminal, another vaulting wonder of Moroccan Moderne, complete with a pizzeria and a Virgin record store that stocked a generous selection of Gnawa CDs.

The passengers were frisked and searched six times before boarding the RAM 767 – which was packed to the overhead bins – for the Atlantic crossing. I fell asleep ten minutes after leaving the sea-sprayed coast of Morocco behind, and woke up seven hours later in New York. An hour after that, I was driving toward Manhattan on the Van Wyck Expressway, and wondering if my soulful sojourn in Le Rouge had been just a kif dream. On Long Island in mid-May, the parkway sparkled with new green growth. My Marrakech desert eyes were bedazzled by the abrupt change from red.

ALLAH ATIC SAHA

This first printing of *To Marrakech by Aeroplane* is limited to 150 copies.

Also Available from Inkblot

Brion Gysin
Living with Islam

This recently discovered manuscript is as relevant today or more so than when it was written. A superb account of the intricacies and philosophy of Muslims and the Islamic world.

ISBN 0 934301 50 6

$12

Available from:
Aftermath Books
42 Forest St.
Providence, Rhode Island
02906

www.ingramcontent.com/pod-product-compliance
Lightning Source LLC
Chambersburg PA
CBHW031209090426
42736CB00009B/852